disintegration

poems by

Paul Robert Mullen

For Barbara
"Happy Birthday"

- 2020 -

lack engenders polished self-regard. These deft, sparse poems, like winter trees, stand stark against what might be sunrise or sunset, but offer an assured quiet voice, in a variety of moods, not all elegiac. Their artifice is worn lightly, in line-break and lineation, in apposite image: you can feel those 'spider-web-december snowflakes'. Similes surprise, with what could be an embrace or menace: 'words/climbing on me/like fingers over the shoulder'. They counsel their readers into people who 'have poetry'."

Robert Sheppard – British poet and critic,
author of *Twentieth Century Blues*

"Paul Robert Mullen's *disintegration* is itself "a thickening of senses," pointing our attention to rust smell, objects that fizzle and sizzle, and light in many forms: candles, gold, sun, and headlights piercing through "rains and hauntings." Sensory images, including "burying pennies" and "the slow melt of butterflies," ground abstract inquiries that continue to haunt creative types—why depth of feeling seems to set one apart, and whether one is living to write or writing to live. In my favorite poem, "after school," the speaker asks why a friend entrusted him with a story about UFOs. Like the friend in the poem, Mullen knows his audience will follow where he leads: "it's because you believed me.""

Sarah Lyn Rogers – American poet,
Editorial Director for Society of Young Inklings
and author of *Inevitable What*

"*disintegration* both lets the world in and keeps it at a distance. Mullen's lens puts relationships, landscapes, current events, and even the past at arm's length, letting the reader graze his poems with the tips of their fingers. The tactile nature of the images in this book tells a story of deep knowing, expectation, and even maybe a tinge of regret. In the opening lines of the book, the reader is told to 'wait', but then immediately is satiated. That satisfaction carries through the rest of the poems in a journey of discovery."

Sage Danielle Curtis – American poet,
author of *Trashcan Funeral*

"In *disintegration*, Paul Robert Mullen's poems paint beautiful and devastating portraits of heartbreak and holding. These small, but illuminated poems are powerful examples of craft and intent; the space created, a landscape of memory- shared."

Alexus Erin, American poet,
author of *St. John's Wort* and *Two Birds, All Moon*

also by Paul Robert Mullen:

curse this blue raincoat (2017)

testimony (2018)

35 (2018)

Paul
Robert
Mullen

disintegr
a
t
i
o
n

ANIMAL HEART PRESS

It takes the heart of an animal

Mullen/Paul Robert, author

disintegration / Paul Robert Mullen

Poems

ISBN: 978-1-67801-899-3

Edited by: Elisabeth Horan
Book Design: Amanda McLeod
Cover Art: adapted from a photograph by Philippe Mignot via Unsplash.
Used with permission.
Crack effect brushes created by FrostBo via DeviantArt.
Cover Design: Amanda McLeod

Animal Heart Press
Thetford Center, VT 05075
Website: www.animalheartpress.net
Email: animalheartpress@gmail.com

dedicated to the lovers who lose but try to love again

table of contents

images

wait until you see yourself

in spring lake

    reflections

in the luminous heavy looking glass

in spiralling winds

      on plains in april

    as months shift

like blackbirds preparing broods in colour

you will see yourself in teardrops

in autumnal mists

    over russet meadows

in spider-web-december snowflakes

in the first tomorrow

    you'll ever remember

dreamcave

the candlelight

at the back of the garden

somehow reminds me

    of you

i watch it burn deep into dreams

dancing on the zephyr

    to the tinkle of wind-chimes

watch fire

bleed & rise onto cold stone

take myself to bed

        alone

lament

are these words

formed out of remembering?

    memories

like bronze in an early winter sunset

clinging to trees

those things you said

         words

    climbing on me

like fingers over the shoulder

a coin in the wishing well

    reflections in weighty shimmering silver

    little kids watching with expressions

way beyond their years

signs

the bullywhip of voices in the hall

    woke us

light formations on diamond tiles

shadows under the door

the next day / blossom under branches

    faces in the woods

figures shifting // shapes & rare imaginings

you said they were here and a part of me

    believed it

i didn't say goodbye

    before i drove toward the coast

watching from the window

images fizzing

across junctions between

      nerve cells

the shoreline beautiful during storms

chemical changes   in the air

some kind of diffusion

the aftermath   of events   that should never

      have happened

the light   seems dense

a thickening of senses

      rust smell from the

         temporary heater

i pull out the notebooks   the pen

      but the words aren't there

days

mother said

why are you wasting your days

writing poetry?

why are you spending your life

in coffee shops

      squandering your best years?

why don't you

      get over that girl?

she was no good for you anyway

i told her

i never chose to be a poet

if i could

i'd have been a bird

      and she shrugged in such a way

that the days became heavier

than the sun

some people have no poetry

what do they *do*?

do they ever go to see

the storms stroke the heads

of apartment blocks?

what do they reach for when winter

raps the windows

      in late november

comes through the door huddled in sheepskin

      puts his bags down

            and smiles?

how do they look into the eyes

of another

and see anything but just

         themselves?

dark corners

couldn't we have waited for the gold

      through the rain?

couldn't we have searched the halo

through the overcast skies

      the rotting menageries

the floods?

couldn't we have found that candlelight

in the garden

      long before i wrote about it?

      couldn't we?

sundown over shadowlands

i was left wondering

if the sunlight would ever make it

   through the keyhole

if i would ever hear voices again

if anybody sat in the pub

   on saturday afternoons

in front of TV screens and horses

would recall my name

   our names

if the bus-stops in the villages

even exist anymore

now that we roll towards something

   entirely different

     than one another

truth & lies

father told me that people who

tell lies never prosper

i believed him for years

until the reflections in photographs

on mantelpieces

on bookcases

on walls

      taught me that truth

          amounts to nothing

      but pain

after school

we laughed about UFO's at the end of class

your dad had seen one

      over the moors east of the village

you smiled and told me you were walking home

we stopped at the crossroads between

shirdley hill & the bypass

      to pick gooseberries from farmland

it's because you believed me

      you said when i asked you

why me?

i'd never felt so alive

postcards from 1999

it's all a journey

a fear of losing

      losing multiplies

like numbers

careering into future moments

dragging the past

      under the wheels

memories

strobes in the pleasuredome

      silence on the streets at dawn

watching headlights

      slog through rains

hauntings

      that we endure

chain

the daisy chain hasn't long broken

you sit beneath the crack willow

     reading poems

by Maya Angelou

i'm fixing it   i grin

     twisting them round thumb and finger

fix it so it'll never break

     you whisper

firecrests

nibs of blood

plumed on the edges of your

      fingernails

i held you –

      so much gestured

so little understood

someday we won't know one another

      you slurred

      almost inaudible

dressed in yellow

      you were in bloom

the slow melt of butterflies

into the nakedness of shadows

into dirty blood-axe greens

birds captive in sizzling sallow tulips calling

      into catkins

calling into

calling

that time i just couldn't ask

through foam

      our toes

gull-threaded surfs curl around border lights

your hair the flush of blood

a mistress of dance

      moving through solid air & space

reserved for something still

      waves gaining urgency

my questions hanging   on the edge of now

down the line

it is 4am

dawn climbs her infinite horizons

i am drunk / disheveled

      amidst the milky rising light

dawn chorus peeling

         skin from under deepened eyes

i see it like a movie in space & time

powder exploding

      a terrible dream

drowning in glory & fag ends

you ask me where i want to go

i say *wherever you are going*

innards

you are the part of me

they cannot see

on scans

i've had it here   you say

      though i can't believe it

the spice upon my upper lip

      tremor down the backbone

fuck brexit   you laugh

      packing bags

           glowing fingernails

the rust upon my heart strings

      in A-minor

there's more to be had

      zipping seams like violence

motion in my retinas

the clock about to strike the hour

barren

when you have

        nothing left

no curves   no softness

no face staring back in mirrors

no autumn climbing from the pocket

        of summer

when you just *don't*

friday night

the stars   unenviable

       they have to shine

and tonight

the dunes flicker

            through gritted teeth

the boys are partying down the coast

borrowed cars

       ripping tracks into sand

music thumping the moon

sat amongst reeds

       away from headlight allure

i sit burying pennies

nebulas   luminous

       hang above me

headlines

the news said that

across the river

    the convoy had exploded

the news said the dead included teens

    not long enrolled

the news said the families had been

informed and were in

    'a bad place'

the news said nothing about us

i called friends

    told them i should have done this and that

should have said *i need you* more

    walked with you in the mornings

    held you in the evenings

stopped myself when…

    just stopped

when the hearts of two poets break

they write all the things
they hoped they'd never have to

lie down too much

ponder over playlists that exacerbate pain

worship the object with irrational hope

embrace tragedy like a sad-eyed dog

message each other
with encouragement that takes all their strength
as though the buttons on their
cell phones are lined with lead

hurl their hurt at computer screens
with something resembling bravery
something resembling fear
      nothing that is anything less
than truth

we lost you

the search was called off

abandoned

      unjustifiable

peeling gristle from surviving photographs

i changed the channel

      lights from motorcades glancing

            half-open blinds

acknowledgements

'some people have no poetry' was previously published in Issue #1 of *The Broken Spine Artist Collective*

'headlines' was previously published in Issue #2 of *Recenter Press Journal*

from the author

I'd like to thank my family and friends for their constant support.

I'd like to express my immense gratitude to Matthew MC Smith, editor of Black Bough Poetry, for his generous editorial eye over many of these poems in their early forms.

Thanks to Elisabeth Horan, Amanda McLeod and the rest of the team at Animal Heart Press who believe so deeply in my work.

Thanks to all readers who support little known poets.

Paul Robert Mullen

June 2020